CW00530469

This book
belongs to
_____
_____
_____

101 INSPIRATIONS FOR YOUR JOURNEY

Meredith Gaston

LANTERN

an imprint of
PENGUIN BOOKS

Dearest Travellers,

♡

No matter where we may find ourselves right now and how we have chosen to travel life's path up to this very point, we have all been journeying together.

From the moment we wake up in the morning until the stars start their twinkling at night, our days are rich with unique experiences, feelings, and possibilities.

The way we think about ourselves, others, and the world around us creates our daily realities. The laws of attraction are very simple and very real — wonderful, positive thoughts can create wonderful, positive lives!

With this in mind, it makes sense to choose happiness because it is so good for our health and wellbeing! ♡

Indeed, the journey so many of us embark on to 'find' happiness in our day to day lives is about seeking wellbeing - about **feeling good.** Our richest moments are when we feel pure joy buzzing within ourselves, and a sense of connection to other travellers and the world around us.

These wonderful little seeds of joy, moments ever-present in daily life and visible to the mindful heart, start to grow and blossom. Soon our inner gardens become so divine and verdant they will extend beyond ourselves and bring joy to the lives of others.

»

This book is about inviting ourselves to live the most abundant and joyous journeys imaginable. I have gathered beautiful words of wisdom from far and wide to inspire and delight us, and to encourage us to travel thoughtfully and with love for ourselves, life, and each other.

To embrace curiosity and gratitude, and to keep our hearts open from moment to moment, makes us rich and happy travellers upon this earth.

So when you are ready, turn the page and let your very own adventures begin!

With love,
Meredith

x

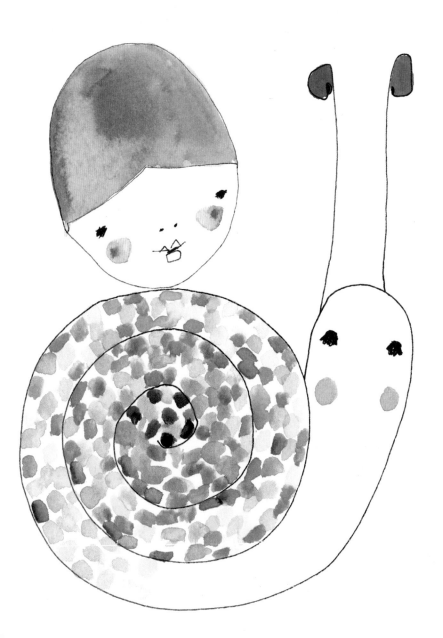

I have decided
to be happy
because
it is good for my
health!

— Inspired by Voltaire —

We do not receive
wisdom,
We must discover it
for ourselves after
a journey through the
wilderness that no one
can take for us.

— Marcel Proust —

Spread love wherever you go. Let no one ever come to you without leaving happier.

Mother Teresa

Throw your dream
into space like a
kite, and you do not
know what it will bring
back, a new life, a new
friend, a new love, a
new country.

Anais Nin

Wandering
reestablishes
the original harmony
which once existed
between ourselves
and the universe.

Anatole France

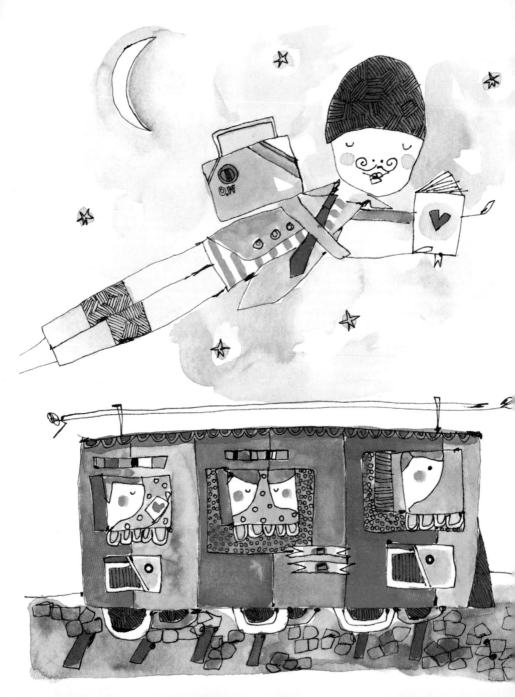

I never travel
without my diary.

One should always
have something
sensational to read
in the train.

Oscar Wilde

The moment that
you realise you
deserve all the
love and joy
in the world,

it is yours.

- Meredith -

If you have built castles in the air, your work need not be lost; that is where they should be. Now Put the foundations under them.

Henry David Thoreau

There are as many worlds
as there are kinds of days,
and as an opal changes its
colours and its fire to match
the nature of a day, so
do I.

— John Steinbeck —

A person
is free the
moment they wish
to be.

Inspired by Voltaire

YOU ARE MADE OF STARS YOU WERE BORN TO SHINE.

- Meredith -

The only true voyage
of discovery, the only
fountain of Eternal
Youth, would be not to
visit strange lands but
to possess other eyes,
to behold the universe
through the eyes of
another, of a hundred
others, to behold the
hundred universes that
each of them beholds,
that each of them is [...]

- Marcel Proust -

Be kind
whenever possible.
It is always
    possible.

Mother Teresa

Wander far and wander wide,

The universe is
on your side.

Meredith

I will not follow
where the path may
lead, but I will go
where there is no path
and I will leave a
trail.

 Muriel Strode

First ask yourself
be still
and listen.

Deep inside you
have the answer,
always.

- Meredith -

Travel makes one
modest. You see
what a tiny place
you occupy in the
world.

— Gustave Flaubert —

Respond
to every call
that excites
your
spirit!

Rumi

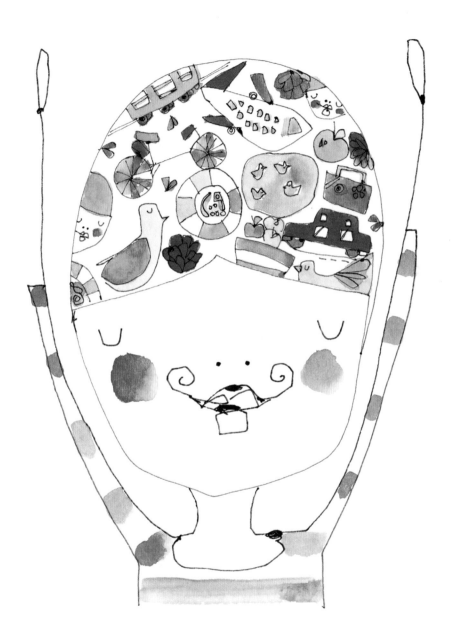

One way to
get the most out
of life is to look
upon it as an
adventure.

— William Feather —

Wherever you are
and whatever you do,
be in Love.

— rumi —

Go on...
Throw all the colour
imaginable onto the
blank canvas of your life!
Paint your world with
love, passion and creativity.
Be unforgettable.

- Meredith -

Don't wait any longer.
DIVE IN THE OCEAN.

Leave
and let the
sea be you.

− Rumi −

The traveller sees
  what he sees.
The tripper sees what
  he has come to see.

G K Chesterton

NOW AT LAST THEY WERE BEGINNING CHAPTER ONE OF THE GREAT STORY WHICH NO ONE ON EARTH HAS READ: WHICH GOES ON FOREVER : IN WHICH EVERY CHAPTER IS BETTER THAN THE ONE BEFORE.

C. S. Lewis

Every day is a
journey,
and the journey itself
is home.

— Mitsuo Basho —

STAND OUT from the crowd.

BE bold
BE different
BE brave
BE you.

- Meredith -

We are given the
GIFT OF LIFE
to honour and
treasure and cherish.

To LIVE WELL is
to open our gift
again and again with
EACH NEW DAY.

— Meredith —

Each
friend

represents a world in us, a world possibly not born until they arrive, and it is only by this meeting that a **new world** is born.

Anais Nin

NEVER TELL ME
THE SKY'S THE
LIMIT,
THERE ARE FOOTPRINTS
ON THE MOON !

Paul Brandt

TO GAIN
ALL WHILE
YOU GIVE,

TO ROAM
THE ROADS
OF LANDS
REMOTE,

TO TRAVEL IS TO LIVE.   Hans Christian Andersen

We never step
in the same river
twice, for it's not
the same river
and we are not
the same people.

– Heraclitus –

You

must be the
change
you wish
to see
in the world.

Anonymous

Simplicity,
patience,
compassion.
These three are your
greatest treasures.

Lao Tzu

We travel the world
over to find our
bliss, yet we often
return home to find
it.

- Meredith -

LOVE
FORGIVE
BE KIND
SUCCEED
BE HONEST
BUILD
BE HAPPY
DO GOOD.

Inspired by
Kent M. Keith

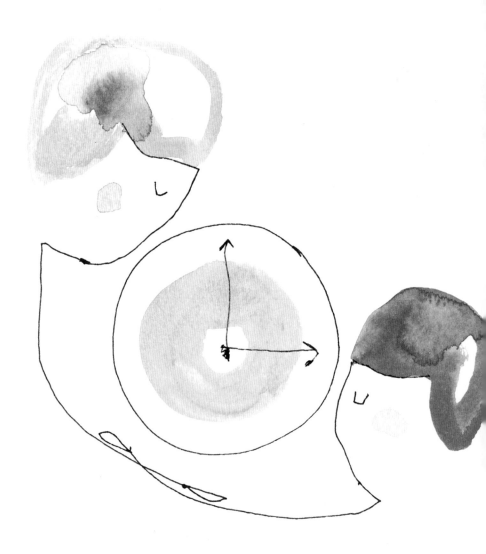

better three
hours too soon
than a minute
too late.

William Shakespeare

adventure.
is not outside
man

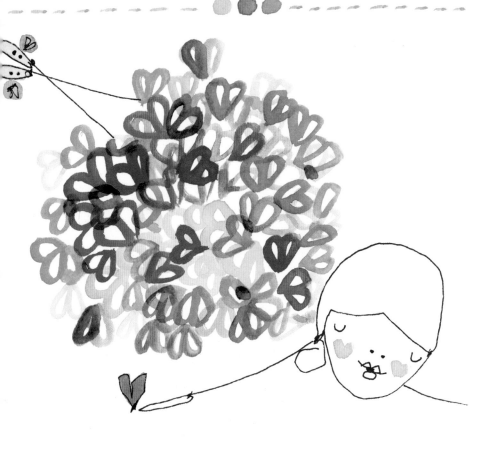

it is within.

George Eliot

Come to the edge.
We might fall.
Come to the edge.
It's too high.

Come TO THE EDGE!

And they came
And he pushed
And they **flew.**

Christopher Logue

the entire universe

is inside you · Rumi

If you want
to be more alive,
Love is the truest
health.

- Rumi -

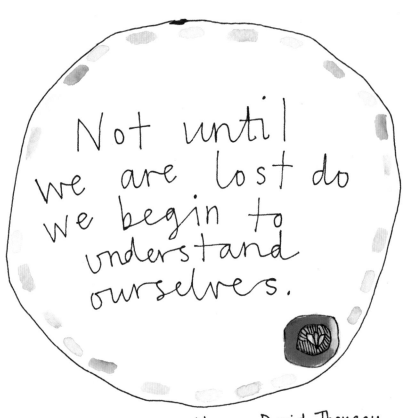

Not until
we are lost do
we begin to
understand
ourselves.

Henry David Thoreau

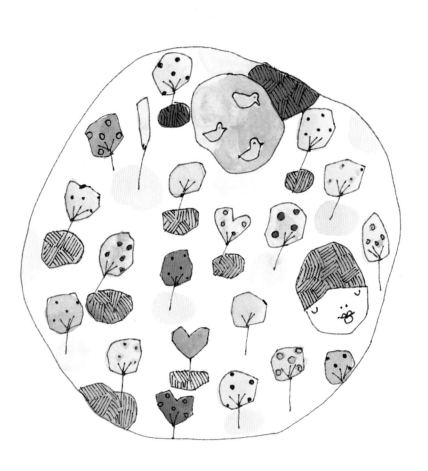

In books I have
travelled, not only
into other worlds but
into my own.

-Anna Quindlen-

I STILL
CLOSE MY EYES
AND GO HOME.

I CAN ALWAYS
DRAW FROM THAT

♥

— Dolly Parton —

To thine
own
self
be
true.

William Shakespeare

Don't be satisfied
with stories,
how things have gone
for others.

Unfold your own myth.

— Rumi —

A good traveller
has no fixed
plans,
and is not intent
on arriving.

Lao Tzu

Always be a
first-rate version of
yourself,
instead of a second-rate
version of somebody
else!

— Judy Garland —

If things are
going untowardly
one month,
they are sure to
mend
the next.

Jane Austen

The future belongs
to those who believe
in the beauty of their
dreams.

Anonymous

For each new morning
with its light,
for rest and shelter of the night,

For health and food, for love and friends,
For everything Thy goodness sends!

Ralph Waldo Emerson

If you
don't like the
road you're walking

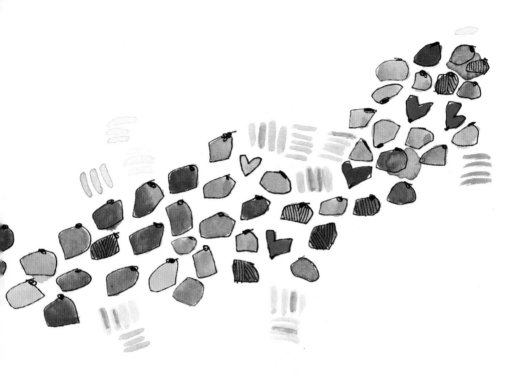

Start paving
another one.

♥ Dolly Parton ♥

Only from
the heart
can you touch
the
sky

– Rumi –

Make Voyages.
Attempt them.
There is nothing
else.

— Tennessee Williams —

The greater danger
for most of us lies
not in setting our aim
too high and falling
short; but in setting our
aim too low and achieving
our mark.

V   - proverb -

If you
wish to
travel far and
fast,

travel light.

Take off all your envies,
jealousies, unforgiveness,
selfishness and fears.

Attributed to Cesare
Pavese

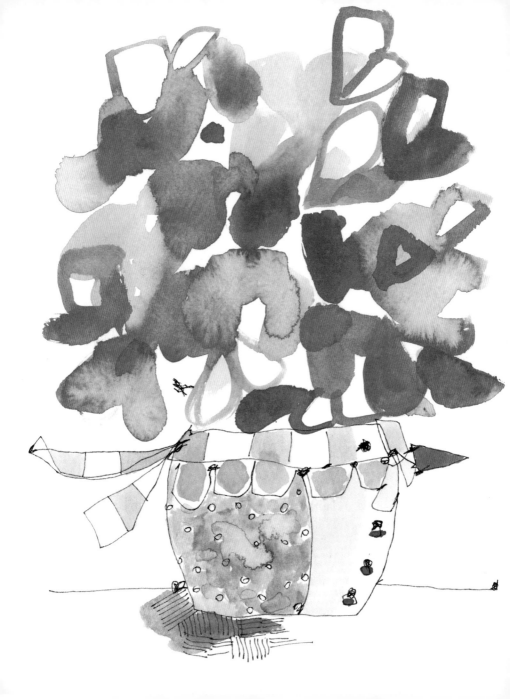

What you
seek is seeking
you.
— Rumi —

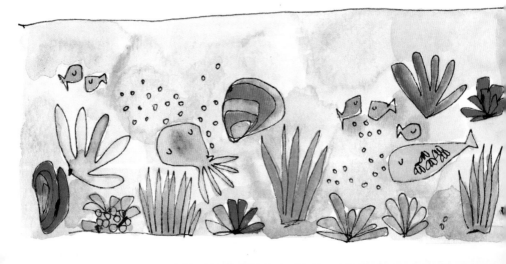

SOMETIMES YOUR ONLY TRANSPORTATION IS A LEAP OF FAITH.

Margaret Shepard

We all have a
better guide in
ourselves, if we
would attend to it,
than any other
person can be.

Jane Austen

The
most
important
decision
you
make ...

is to be in a good mood!

Anonymous ♡

Gratitude can transform common days into thanksgivings, turn routine jobs into joy, and change ordinary opportunities into blessings.

William Arthur Ward

Look past your
thoughts, so you
may drink the pure
nectar of this moment

— Rumi —

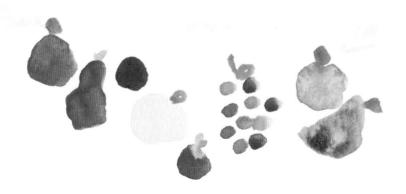

The plain fact is that
the planet does not
need more successful people.

But it does desperately need
more peacemakers, healers,
restorers, storytellers, and
lovers of every kind.

David W. Orr

START A HUGE,
FOOLISH PROJECT,
LIKE NOAH,
IT MAKES ABSOLUTELY
NO DIFFERENCE WHAT
PEOPLE THINK ABOUT
YOU!

— RUMI —

Searching all directions
with one's awareness,
one finds no one dearer
than oneself.

In the same way, others
are fiercely dear
to themselves.

one should not
hurt others
if one loves oneself.

— Buddha —

We should come
home from adventures,
and perils, and discoveries
every day, with new
experience and
character.

Henry David Thoreau

we know
what we are,
but know not what
we may be.

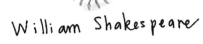

William Shakespeare

Do not let it
be your aim to
be something
but to be
someone.

Victor Hugo

One small
positive
thought in
the morning
can change
your whole day.

·Meredith·

Life shrinks
or expands
according to
one's
courage.

Anais Nin

We don't see things as they are,

we see them as **we** are.

Anonymous

There will
come a time when
you believe everything
is finished.

This will be the
beginning.

Louis L'Amour

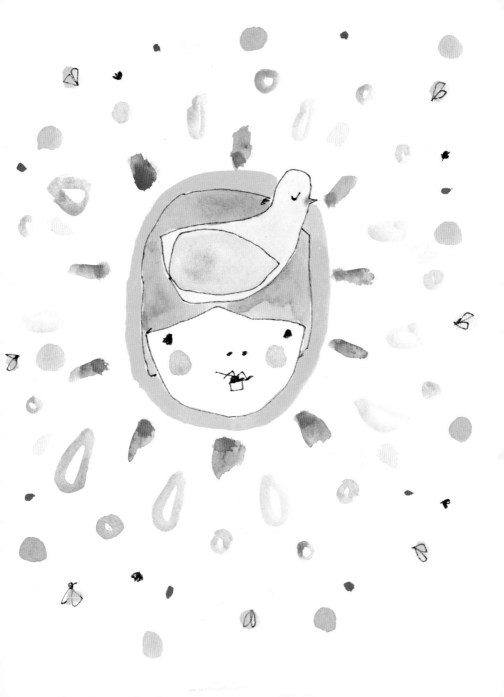

Live,
Love,
and let be.

Anonymous

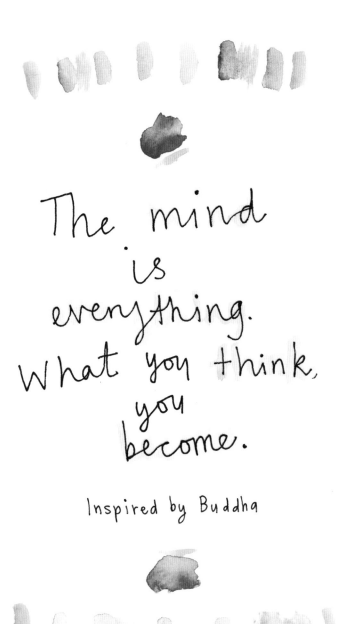

The mind
is
everything.
What you think,
you
become.

Inspired by Buddha

The world is
a book
and those who
do not travel
read only
one page.

Anonymous

Success is
liking yourself,
liking what you do,
and liking
how you do it.

Maya Angelou
♡

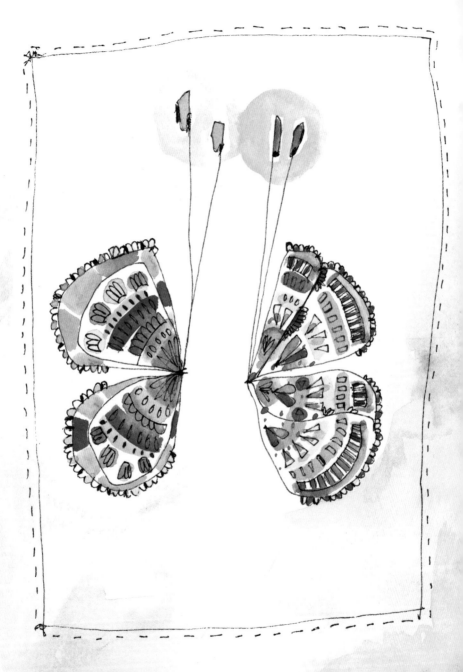

Comparison

is

the thief

of

joy.

Anonymous

Happiness is
when what you
think, what you say
and what you do are
in harmony.

Mahatma
Gandhi

What you **are** is
what you have been.

What you **will be**
is what you do now.

Buddha

PLANS
du jour
1. _____
2. _____
3. _____

It takes as
much energy to
wish
as it does
to plan.

Inspired by Eleanor Roosevelt

People take different
roads to seeking
    fulfilment and
happiness.

Just because they're not
on your road does not
mean they are lost.

- Inspired by The Dalai Lama -

We **live** in the world when we **Love** it.

Rabindranath Tagore

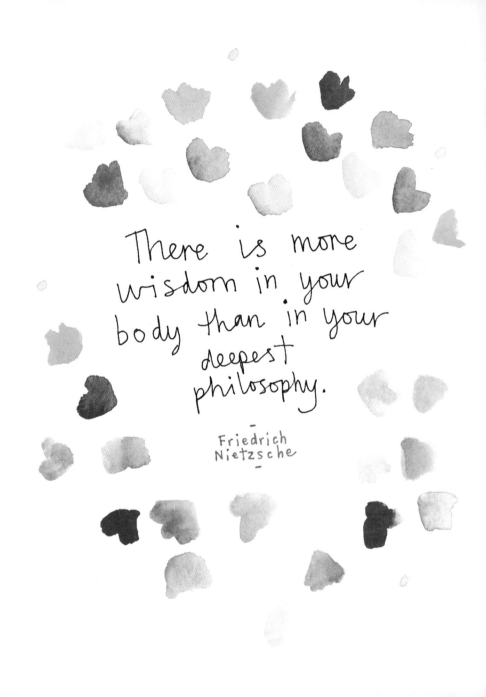

There is more
wisdom in your
body than in your
deepest
philosophy.

Friedrich
Nietzsche

True happiness
comes from the
joy of deeds well
done,
the zest of creating
things
new.

Inspired by Antoine de Saint-
Exupery

I will not let
anyone
walk through my
mind with their
dirty feet.

Inspired by
Mahatma Gandhi

Our deepest fear is not that
we are inadequate.
Our deepest fear is that we
are powerful beyond measure.
It is our light, not our darkness
that frightens us.
We ask ourselves "Who am I
to be brilliant, gorgeous, talented, fabulous?"
Actually, who are you not to be? ...

Your playing small doesn't serve the world.
There is nothing enlightened about shrinking
So that other people won't feel insecure
around you.
We are all meant to shine, as children
do. We are born to manifest the glory
of God that is within us.

It is not in some of us, it is in
everyone.

And as we make our own light
shine,

We unconsciously give others permission
to **do the same.**

As we are liberated from our fear,
our presence automatically liberates
others.

Marianne Williamson

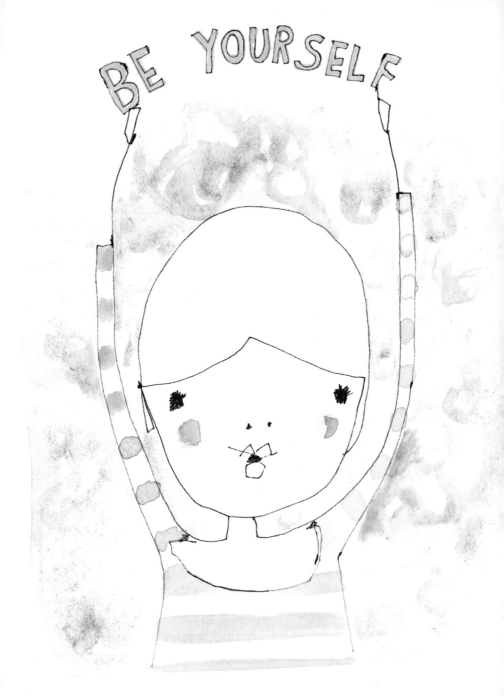

To be yourself
in a world that
is constantly trying
to make you something
else is the greatest
accomplishment.

Inspired by
E . E . Cummings

I live my life in widening circles that reach out across the world.

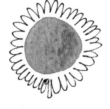

Inspired by Rainer Maria Rilke

A ship in
harbour
is safe,
but that is
not
what ships
are built for.

John A. Shedd

Admiration
and
familiarity
are strangers.

— Inspired by George Sand —

A mind that is
stretched by a new
experience can never
go back to its old
dimensions.

Inspired by Oliver Wendall
Holmes Snr.

No matter

how
hard

the past

you can always begin again.

Jack Kornfield

Travel is more
than the seeing
of things.
It is a change
that goes on, deep
and permanent, in
the ideas
of
living

Miriam Beard

Now and then
it's good to pause in
our pursuit of
happiness and
just
be
happy.

Inspired by
Apollinaire

Life is like riding
a bicycle,

you must
keep
moving!

Albert Einstein

like all
great travellers,
I have seen more
than I remember, and
remember more than I
have seen.

Benjamin Disraeli

Life is not a problem to be solved,

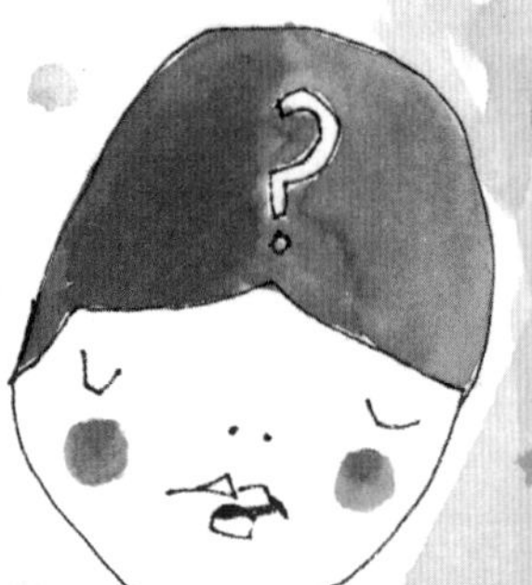

It is
a
reality
to
be
experienced.

Sarvepalli
Radhakrishnan

Life is a series
of natural and
spontaneous changes.
Don't resist them, that
only creates sorrow.
Let reality be reality.
Let things flow naturally
forward in whatever way
they like.

Lao Tzy

think a
bit

differently.

If everyone is
thinking alike,
then no one is
thinking.

Inspired by
Benjamin Franklin

Anyone who
lives within their
means suffers from
a lack of
imagination.

—

Inspired by
Oscar Wilde

The things that
make me different are
the things that
make me

me.

Inspired by A.A. Milne

The best
is yet
to come.

popular saying

Thank you

My life is full of joy, love and adventure, and this little book represents my big, deep gratitude to those who brighten my world. ☆

To my publisher Lantern, Penguin, with special love to Julie Gibbs, Katrina O'Brien, Emily O'Neill and Jocelyn Hungerford, to my dear friends and family who inspire and amaze me, and to my beloved Mr. Lindemann who I met on an unforgettable journey, and with whom I fell in love at first sight. (At an airport, of all places!)

》

I thank you too, reader, for sharing in these pages and for allowing them to brighten your onward travels.

I dedicate this book with my heart to my Grandmother Nora, my inspiration and fellow gypsy. I will love her all my days. ♡

x m

LANTERN

Published by the Penguin Group
Penguin Group (Australia)
707 Collins Street, Melbourne, Victoria, 3008, Australia
(A division of Pearson Australia Group Pty Ltd)
Penguin Group (USA) Inc.
375 Hudson Street, New York, New York 10014, USA
Penguin Group (Canada)
90 Elgington Avenue East, Suite 700, Toronto, Canada, ON M4P 2Y3
(A division of Pearson Penguin Canada Inc.)
Penguin Books Ltd
80 Strand, London WC2R 0RL England
Penguin Ireland
25 St Stephens Green, Dublin 2, Ireland
(a division of Penguin Books Ltd)
Penguin Books India PVT Ltd
11 Community Centre, Panchsheel Park, New Delhi - 110 017, India
Penguin Group (NZ)
67 Apollo Drive, Rosedale, Auckland 0632, New Zealand
(A division of Pearson New Zealand Ltd)
Penguin Books (South Africa) (Pty) Ltd, Rosebank Office Park, Block D
181 Jan Smuts Avenue, Parktown North, Johannesburg 2196 South Africa
Penguin (Beijing) Ltd
7F, Tower B, Jiaming Center, 27 East Third Ring Road North,
Chaoyang District, Beijing 100020, China

Penguin Books Ltd, Registered Offices: 80 Strand, London,
WC2R 0RL, England

First published by Penguin Group (Australia) 2015

1 2 3 4 5 6 7 8 9 10

Text copyright © Meredith Gaston 2015.
Illustrations copyright © Meredith Gaston 2015
The moral right of the author has been asserted.

All rights reserved. Without limiting the rights under
copyright reserved above, no part of this publication
may be reproduced, stored in or introduced into a retrieval
system, or transmitted, in any form or by any means
(electronic, mechanical, photocopying, recording or otherwise)
without the prior written permission of both the copyright
owner and the above publisher of this book.

Cover and text design by Emily O'Neill © Penguin Group (Australia)
Illustrations by Meredith Gaston
Colour separation by Splitting Image Colour studio, Clayton, Victoria.
Printed and bound in China by Hung-Hing Offset Printing Co. Ltd.

National Library of Australia
Cataloguing-in-Publication data:

101 Inspirations for your journey / Meredith Gaston.
9781921384004 (hardback)
Inspiration - Quotations, maxims, etc.
Travel - Quotations, maxims, etc.
Voyages and travel - Quotations, maxims, etc.
808.882

penguin.com.au/lantern

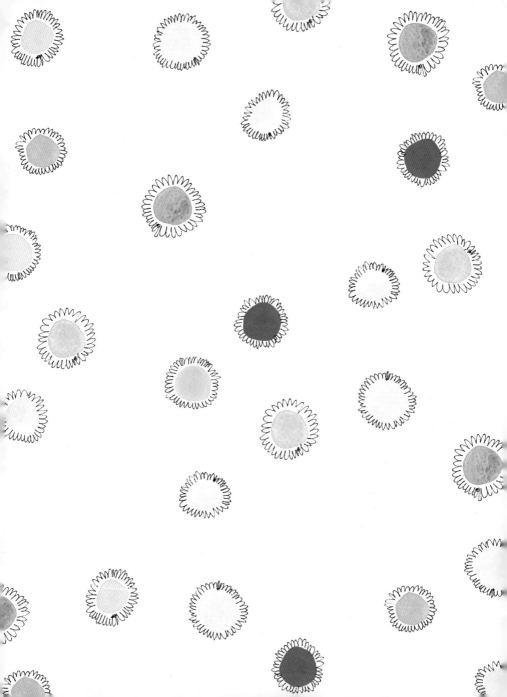